Novels for Students, Volume 2

Since this page cannot legibly accommodate all copyright notices, the acknowledgments constitute an extension of the copyright notice.

and other applicable laws. The authors and editors of this work have added value to the underlying factual material herein through one or more of the following: unique and original selection, coordination, expression, arrangement, and classification of the information.

All rights to this publication will be vigorously defended.

This book is printed on acid-free paper that meets the minimum requirements of American National Standard for Information Sciences—Permanence Paper for Printed Library Materials, ANSI Z39.48-1984.

ISBN 0-7876-1687-7
ISSN 1094-3552

Printed in the United States of America
10 9 8 7 6 5 4

One Flew Over the Cuckoo's Nest

Ken Kesey 1962

Introduction

Ken Kesey's tragicomic novel, One *Flew Over the Cuckoo's Nest*, takes place in a mental hospital during the late 1950s. The book can be read on two levels; if one looks on the surface, there is the story of how a highly individualistic, near-superman named McMurphy becomes a patient and for a time overturns the senseless and dehumanizing routines of the ward. If one looks deeper, however, there is a commentary on U.S. society, which the Beat generation of the late 1950s viewed as so hopelessly conformist as to stifle individuality and creativity.

First published in 1962, Kesey's book bridges the transition from the Beatniks of the late 1950s, who used poetry, music, and fashion to express their dissatisfaction with conformist society, to the hippies of the 1960s, whose counterculture rebellion included free love and drug use. Because *Cuckoo's Nest* was both timely and provocative, it became an instant hit with critics and with a college generation that was ready to take on the establishment full-tilt. Over the years, the book has enjoyed many reprintings in paperback form. It started receiving scholarly attention in the 1970s, particularly after it was made into an Academy Award-winning movie of the same title starring Jack Nicholson, who gave a brilliant performance as the irrepressible McMurphy. Although the novel has sometimes been faulted as sexist and racist, it still endures as an example of the individual's battle not to succumb to the forces of a dehumanizing, demoralizing society.

Author Biography

Ken Kesey was born in 1935 in LaJunta, Colorado. The family moved to Springfield, Oregon, where he attended public school before attending and graduating from the University of Oregon. While in college, he pursued drama and athletics. A champion wrestler, he nearly won a place on the U.S. Olympic team. After graduating, he worked for a year, thought about becoming a movie actor, and wrote an unpublished novel about college athletics entitled "End of Autumn." Kesey married his high-school sweetheart, Faye Haxy, in 1956, and the couple became the parents of three children. In 1958, Kesey began graduate work in creative writing at Stanford University in California, where he studied with several noted writers, including novelist Wallace Stegner. He wrote a second unpublished novel, "Zoo," before beginning *One Flew Over the Cuckoo's Nest* in the summer of 1960. Around this time, he became a paid volunteer in government-sponsored drug experiments at the Veteran's Hospital in Menlo Park, California. There he was introduced to psychoactive drugs such as mescaline and LSD, and became a frequent user of them. He was under the influence of these drugs during some of the time he wrote this, his first published novel.

Cuckoo's Nest enjoyed considerable critical and popular success after its 1962 publication, becoming especially popular on college campuses.

Kesey himself gained additional notoriety with a group of friends who titled themselves the "Merry Pranksters" and travelled the country promoting the new "counterculture" of social protest and psychedelic drugs. The experiences of Kesey and his friends were chronicled in Tom Wolfe's noted 1968 work *The Electric Kool-Aid Acid Test.* This trip was not without cost, however, for Kesey was arrested in 1965 for drug possession and eventually spent about five months in jail and in the San Mateo County Sheriff's Honor Camp. Released in 1967, he moved back to Oregon in 1968, taking up residence on a farm in Pleasant Hills. He gave up writing for a period of time before returning to his former art. He also kicked his drug habit successfully, and has since disavowed experimental drug use, saying "There are dues." None of his subsequent works have received the same attention as *Cuckoo's Nest*, which is seen as both a predecessor to and representative of the counterculture movement of the 1960s.

Plot Summary

Part 1

One Flew Over the Cuckoo's Nest is the story of a few remarkable weeks in an Oregon insane asylum and the events that lead to the narrator's escape. A tall and broad Indian, Chief Bromden is a long-term inmate who tells the story. His insanity appears to stem from a paranoid belief in the existence of a machine, "The Combine," which controls people's behavior. He feigns deafness and dumbness in order to fight this control. In looking back on his time in the ward, he finds that he must recount the horrible experiences suffered by him and his fellow inmates. In particular he tells of the conflict between Randle McMurphy and Big Nurse Ratched.

Bromden's story begins with the day McMurphy is first admitted to the ward. McMurphy is loud and disruptive, and introduces himself as a gambling man who has only pretended to be crazy in order to get out of a work camp. He introduces himself to the "Chronics" (permanent residents), including Bromden himself, and the "Acutes" (who may still recover). McMurphy immediately attempts to take charge of the bunch by instigating a who-is-crazier-than-whom debate with Harding, an Acute who is president of the Patients Council.

Nurse Ratched knows that McMurphy

represents a disruptive force on the ward, and Bromden explains her reaction to disruptive forces:

> The big nurse tends to get real put out if something keeps her outfit from running like a smooth, accurate, precision-made machine. The slightest thing messy or out of kilter or in the way ties her into a little white knot of tight-smiled fury. She walks around with that same doll smile crimped between her chin and her nose and that same calm whir coming from her eyes, but down inside of her she's tense as steel. I know, I can feel it. And she don't relax a hair till she gets the nuisance attended to—what she calls "adjusted to surroundings."

McMurphy questions the others, particularly Harding, about why they accept her power over them. He bets the entire ward that within a week he can force Nurse Ratched to lose control without her gaining any over him.

Interspersed with his own hallucinations, Bromden recounts how McMurphy persistently taunts the Nurse and her attendants. Some ward-members gain access to an old hydrotherapy room —the "tub room"— to escape the very loud music in the day room. In an effort to motivate the Acutes into fighting Big Nurse, McMurphy purposefully loses a wager that he can heave an old concrete console through a tub room window and escape.

One week after the original bet, he succeeds in turning the entire ward against Ratched in a vote over television privileges during the World Series. Bromden's is the decisive vote, and McMurphy gains the majority he needs to win. The nurse refuses to turn the television on, but the entire ward ignores her orders and sits patiently in front of the blank set while she screams hysterically.

Part 2

In response to her failure, Nurse Ratched decides to wait until McMurphy realizes his fate is ultimately in her hands. At the same time, Bromden grows stronger from McMurphy's tireless example, hallucinating less and avoiding his medication. The other patients follow suit, growing more unruly and argumentative.

One day while swimming at the hospital pool, a lifeguard/inmate explains to McMurphy the danger of being permanently committed. As a result, McMurphy's unruliness seems to end. The other patients are not surprised by his change in attitude and recognize that he wants to avoid being committed. Bromden's mechanistic hallucinations return, however, and although Cheswick claims to understand McMurphy's attitude, he kills himself at the bottom of the swimming pool.

In the days following this last incident, McMurphy learns more about the contradictions of medication and other forms of treatment at the hospital. He sees the dilemma faced by epileptics regarding their medication. Harding and Billy Bibbit explain not only the horrors of shock treatment and lobotomy, but also reveal that they are voluntary detainees of the mental hospital. McMurphy is angry and confused at these revelations. When Big Nurse takes away the ward's tub room privileges in an attempt to cement her victory, McMurphy responds by smashing the window that separates the Nurse's Station from the day room.

Part 3

In the days that follow, McMurphy continues to harass the nurse by organizing a deep-sea fishing expedition for the ward. Bromden's hallucinations recede once more, and he begins to think about joining the salmon-fishing list. He worries again about disclosing his ability to hear and talk, but eventually speaks to McMurphy almost without realizing it. McMurphy helps to build the Chiefs confidence by signing his name to the fishing list, and by convincing him that he can once again feel tall and strong—strong enough, in fact, to lift the cement console in the tub room.

McMurphy surpasses several hurdles while the appointed fishing-day approaches. When one of the prostitutes hired to take them to the boat doesn't show up, McMurphy even convinces the hospital's Doctor Spivey to drive half of them to the boat and join them fishing. Along the way, they encounter unfriendly outsiders and the group awaits

McMurphy's leadership to turn their morale around.

As they set sail in the fishing boat with the obsessive-compulsive George Sorensen at the helm, McMurphy reveals that the boat owner, Captain Block, has been duped, and that they will be renting the boat without his permission. After a spectacular day, Captain Block and the police await them at the docks. Doctor Spivey discourages legal action by disputing local jurisdiction and the safety of the boat. The catcallers who insulted the group upon their first arrival are humbled by the success of the fishing expedition. During the drive back to the hospital, Billy Bibbit and Candy sit together, and McMurphy encourages a clandestine late-night "date" between the innocent Billy and the prostitute at the hospital. Thus inspired, they pause in front of the house in which McMurphy was raised while he brags about his first sexual experience.

Part 4

Nurse Ratched's response to McMurphy's success is to try to turn the men on the ward against him by demonstrating how much money he has taken from them since his arrival. As the Chief's confidence grows and, with McMurphy's help, he begins to recognize his own physical size and strength, and the bet regarding the cement console in the tub room is revived. McMurphy makes a bet that it is possible for a man to lift the console, and Bromden lifts it. McMurphy attempts to compensate the Chief with a piece of the winnings, but Bromden becomes upset, saying of McMurphy's activities on the ward, "we thought it wasn't to be *winning* things!"

When Big Nurse orders that the men be cleaned with a special liquid because of vermin they may have encountered on their fishing trip, a fight breaks out. Sorensen is compulsively clean and cannot bear the thought of having the strong smelling disinfectant on (or in) his body. The attendants persist and McMurphy picks a fight with one of them. When the other attendants join in, Bromden enters the fray and settles it decisively in favor of the ward. They thus provide Nurse Ratched with the excuse she needs, and she sends both of the men to the "Disturbed" ward, where they face electroshock therapy. McMurphy refuses to concede victory to Ratched by admitting his fault and undergoes several shock treatments.

Eventually, the day for Billy and Candy's late-night date arrives. The ward prepares by bribing Turkle, the night orderly, and Candy arrives with her friend Sandy in tow. A great party ensues, and although McMurphy's plan is to escape with girls before morning, the entire ward drunkenly falls asleep until discovered the next morning. Billy Bibbit and Candy are found naked together in the Seclusion Room, and Nurse Ratched taunts Billy with the prospect of revealing his activities to his mother. Unable to bear this possibility, Billy kills himself while waiting in Doctor Spivey's office. McMurphy, enraged but calm, smashes into the Nurses' Station and attempts to strangle Ratched.

The Nurse is badly shaken in the days that follow, and orders McMurphy's lobotomy. He is wheeled, comatose, to the ward for all to see. Late that night, Bromden suffocates McMurphy, then heaves the cement console through the window and escapes.

Characters

Pete Bancini

A self-pitying patient who suffered brain damage at birth and says he's been dead for all of his fifty-five years. Constantly complaining of being tired, at times he is forcibly removed from group therapy session and put to bed. As the book unfolds, however, Bancini begins to escape the imprisonment of his fixation on the past and take a more active role in the ward.

Billy Bibbit

A weak mama's boy who is totally under Big Nurse's thumb. She has extra control over him because she has befriended his mother, who works for the hospital. Billy's most notable feature is his severe stutter, which he says he's had since he said his first word: "M-m-m-m-mamma." His mother still treats him as a child, even though he is over thirty years old, and he has problems dealing with women. He eventually begins to assert some limited independence, and loses his virginity with one of McMurphy's girls. But in the end, he becomes victim to Nurse Ratched's manipulation and commits suicide.

Big Nurse

See Nurse Ratched

The Three Black Boys

How Chief refers to the black men who come in early, clean the ward, and herd the patients around according to Nurse Ratched's orders. They hate the nurse, who manipulates them, and take their frustration out on the inmates, often taunting them and otherwise taking advantage of them. McMurphy finally comes to blows with them after they torture Rub-a-Dub George with threats of dirt and bugs. The one-dimensional depiction of these characters has been faulted as racist and stereotypical by several critics.

Chief Bromden

Chief Bromden is the schizophrenic narrator of story, and has been in the mental institution since leaving the Army shortly after World War II. Harding says he's heard that Chief has received over two hundred shock treatments. The son of an American Indian father and a Caucasian mother, he attributes his shrewdness to his Native American heritage. Chief has a paranoid belief in something he calls the "Combine," a collaboration of governmental and industrial groups he believes are trying to control people by way of machines. For many years, Chief has isolated himself from the bizarre environment of the Chronic and Acute ward by pretending to be deaf and dumb. This way, he finds out everything he wants to know and yet is able to keep his own counsel and stay out of trouble.

Chief pushes a broom all day, sweeping the same territory over and over again. He's classified as a Chronic: "Not in the hospital, these, to get fixed, but just to keep them from walking about the street giving the product a bad name," muses Chief. "Chronic are in for good ... divided into Walkers like me, can still walk around if you keep fed, and Wheelers and Vegetables." Chief harbors a deep hatred of the Big Nurse, Miss Ratched, and like all the other ward residents fears her power. Chief holds an almost equal anger at the three black assistants who do Miss Ratched's icy bidding—and worse. (In fact, some consider the book racist because of the negative way in which author—and his narrator storyteller—portray these black characters.)

Chief imagines that every day the staff creates a fog that hangs over the ward. Sometimes the fog is smoke because he believes that walls are wired and filled with humming mechanisms. But he snaps to awareness when a new admission, the irrepressible, irreverent McMurphy, arrives and immediately tries to take over as boss of the ward. At first, Chief is able to hide behind his feigned deafness and just watch McMurphy's antics. But McMurphy soon tricks him into revealing to him that he can both hear and speak—a secret guarded from everyone else. Gradually, under McMurphy's influence, Chief begins to withdraw from his hallucinatory world and begins to join the other residents in activities, even joining them on a fishing expedition.

At one point, he thinks to himself: "I noticed vaguely that I was getting so's I could see some good in the life around me. McMurphy was teaching me. I was feeling better than I'd remembered feeling since I was a kid, when everything was good and land still singing kids' poetry to me." Finally he reveals the source of the book's title, a singsong chant his grandmother used to say as they played a finger game: "one flew east, one flew west, one flew over the cuckoo's nest... O-U-T spells out... goose swoops down and plucks *you* out." Although McMurphy's power over Nurse Ratched eventually ends, his sacrifice serves as an inspiration for Chief. Chief takes pity on McMurphy after he is left a vegetable from a lobotomy, smothering him with a pillow, and then leaves the institution to take control of his own destiny.

Media Adaptations

- A play version of *One Flew Over the Cuckoo's Nest* was written by Dale Wasserman and appeared on Broadway with Kirk Douglas as McMurphy in 1963; the play was revived in 1971. Published by Samuel French, 1970.

- An acclaimed film version of *Cuckoo's Nest* appeared in 1975, starring Jack Nicholson as McMurphy and Louise Fletcher as Nurse Ratched. Named best film of the year at the Academy Awards, the film also won Oscars for the two leads, as well as director Milos Forman and screenwriter Bo Goldman. It is available from Republic Pictures Home Video.

Chief Broom

See Chief Bromden

Charles Cheswick

Supposedly tough and aggressive, Cheswick is actually afraid to take any definitive actions. Faced with a challenge, he makes noise as if he will attack, but he always backs down. But he likes to cheer others on from the sidelines, and soon becomes an enthusiastic supporter of McMurphy's ideas. Soon after making a fuss when McMurphy won't protest against Nurse Ratched's cigarette rationing, Cheswick drowns in the swimming pool, something Big Nurse blames on McMurphy.

Ellis

A Chronic who was an Acute before undergoing shock treatment, Ellis is "nailed" to the wall in a position that recalls Christ's crucifixion.

Mr. Fredrickson

Sefelt's friend and protector, he worries about having epileptic fits and secretly takes Sefelt's medicine for him. After McMurphy is sent from the ward, he and Sefelt sign out of the hospital together.

Mr. Dale Harding

Mr. Harding is president of the Patient's Council. Intelligent, college-educated, he speaks to his fellow-patients like a professor. McMurphy takes him on verbally right away, saying he wants to displace him as the "bull goose loony" who runs things. Harding pretends to compete, but gives McMurphy his position as king of the card games. Harding, while articulate and assertive, is basically like a frightened child, and waves his overly pretty hands when he gets upset. His psychological problems include the inferiority and insecurity he feels because of his young, sexy wife, who continually casts doubts on his manhood. He submits to Big Nurse's verbal humiliations during the group therapy sessions unprotestingly. McMurphy tells Harding these sessions are like pecking parties, in which a flock of chickens rip one of their own to shreds, but Harding refuses to believe that Big Nurse does not intend to help him with these sessions. Under McMurphy's influence, Harding gradually begins to see the truth—that the Big Nurse is slowly emasculating the patients. When the Nurse lies to him about McMurphy's return, he checks himself out of the hospital.

Mrs. Vera Harding

Dale Harding's attractive wife, who has been the subject of many of Big Nurse's group-therapy meetings because Harding thinks Vera may be cheating on him. She makes a brief appearance on a cursory visit to her husband in the hospital, during which she flirts with many of the staff and inmates and casts doubts on her husband's manhood. Later, Harding returns home to her.

Martini

One the patients who often seems to be suffering hallucinations, a fact McMurphy uses to cheat against him in Monopoly.

Colonel Matterson

The oldest Chronic on the ward, a World War I veteran who lectures the other inmates by reading from his palm.

Randle Patrick McMurphy

McMurphy bursts on the well-ordered, claustrophobic scene of the psychiatric ward like a psychological bombshell. Streetwise, smart, aggressive, vigorous, he challenges the status quo—the "way things are"—from day one. He introduces himself to everyone in the ward, shaking hands and filling the silence with loud laughter. Is this man mentally ill? Probably not. He has elected to be sent to the psychiatric hospital because he did not like to work on the prison farm, where he had six months to go before his release. His crime: statutory rape of a willing fifteen year old. The attraction of the psychiatric hospital for him was the idea of enjoying better meals and an easier lifestyle. This is not exactly what he finds.

McMurphy immediately engages in a long, hopeless, and endless battle with Big Nurse, a classic control freak. What McMurphy has brought to the ward is a touch of normalcy. What Nurse Ratched wants is a group of docile and quiet men who do not upset or question how she has ordered things. It is their incarceration, voluntary or otherwise, upon which her job and role in life depends. Therefore McMurphy is the ultimate threat —a nonconformist who stirs the residents into a desire for action. He wakes them up out of the dullness and quiet in which they have been dwelling. In fact, he provides them with the beginning of a cure to their problems.

The more successful McMurphy is at upsetting the status quo, the more intense the battle becomes between him and Nurse Ratched. He takes over as boss of the endless poker game played by some of the Acutes. He also demands in group therapy meetings that democracy reign and that Nurse Ratched loosen up some of the ties that bind the residents to a senseless, rigid schedule that only serves to dehumanize them.

McMurphy is a very funny character. But the humor ends when he discovers that Big Nurse has total control over his fate—over what treatment he receives and when he is discharged—because he is one of the two residents who have been committed. The other is Chief, McMurphy's best friend. What starts as a rollicking rebellion against authority becomes a tragedy. McMurphy is repeatedly subjected to electric shock therapy. He manages to joke about it and to gather the strength to organize a fishing expedition for some of the men. His final challenge is a party at night in the ward that turns into a fiasco. The drunken orgy, complete with prostitutes, is McMurphy's demise. Big Nurse finally pulls the plug and sends him for psychosurgery. He returns, lobotomized, as a human vegetable. All the lights in this bright mind and brave personality have been extinguished. His energizing influence on the residents lives on, however. Several leave to go home after McMurphy's demise as their leader, and Chief Bromden escapes from the ward and heads for the country. Despite his final degradation to a vegetative state, he wins the fight for freedom that he has fought so bravely. But the rewards are not his. They belong to his fellow patients.

Old Pete

See Pete Bancini

Miss Pilbow

One of Nurse Ratched's timid assistants, Miss Pilbow has a highly noticeable blood-colored birthmark. Because of Big Nurse's warnings, she is frightened of McMurphy even when he speaks kindly to her.

Public Relation

An obnoxiously jolly public relations man who shows local society matrons around the ward, pointing out how great everything is. He is more concerned with the appearance of the ward than with the quality of life there.

Nurse Ratched

A sexless, rigid caricature of a nurse, Nurse Ratched imposes discipline on her ward with all the fervor of an Army nurse, which she had been. Large, with huge breasts only partially disguised by her ultra-starched white uniform, she nevertheless has a pretty, delicate face that belies her cruelty.

Manipulative to the core, the only thing that really matters to Ratched is her desire to control everything around her—the environment, the staff, the patients. She has rendered the staff doctor who is in charge of the ward helpless and ineffectual. Her methods are subtle: She speaks with the calm voice of reason, dealing with patients as though they are children. Her group therapy sessions are intentionally humiliating to patients. Her agenda clearly is to turn the group members against one another. That protects her from any unified action against her rules and her dominating role. As long as everyone stays in line, she retreats to her safe place—a glassed-in office overlooking the ward.

Chief sums her up mentally as follows: "So after the nurse gets her staff, efficiency locks the ward like a watchman's clock. Everything the guys think and say and do is all worked out months in advance, based on the little notes the nurse makes during the day. This is typed and fed into the machine I hear humming behind the steel door in the rear of the Nurses' Station."

Small wonder that McMurphy becomes the ultimate threat to her tight, close little domain. He demands that the patients be given rights. She believes they have only the rights she decides to give them. Cruel in the extreme, she plays repetitious loud music over the ward's speaker system, successfully drowning out normal conversation. As her battle with McMurphy intensifies, his hatred of her leads him to aggressive actions against her. Finally, he can stand no more.

In his last battle against reasonless authority, he tries to strangle her. That may be the end of both of them, not just McMurphy, for his example inspires several of the inmates to check themselves out of the ward and out of her power.

Nurse Ratched's character has been the subject of much critical discussion and even controversy, for several observers consider her a sexist stereotype of the controlling female.

Rub-a-Dub George

See George Sorenson

Ruckly

A Chronic who is considered one of the ward's "failures." Aggressive and violent before undergoing a lobotomy, now all Ruckly can say is "Fffffuck da wife!"

Sandy

Candy's prostitute friend, who does not make it to the fishing trip, but joins her at the clandestine ward party.

Mr. Scanlon

A stubborn patient preoccupied with explosives who depends on seeing the six o'clock news every day to make sure the country has not been bombed. He is one of the few Acutes who has been committed. He encourages Chief Bromden to leave after the Chief smothers McMurphy.

Mr. Bruce Sefelt

An epileptic, Sefelt is constantly suspicious that his anticonvulsant medication is causing severe medical problems, so he gives his drugs to Fredrickson, who worries about having fits. After McMurphy is sent away for an operation, Sefelt and Fredrickson sign out of the hospital together.

George Sorenson

A "big, toothless knotty old Swede" who has a fetish about cleanliness. When the group goes on a fishing trip organized by McMurphy, George is the captain. It turns out that he skippered a PT boat during World War II and was a fisherman for twenty-five years. After McMurphy's lobotomy, he transfers to another ward.

Dr. Spivey

Dr. Spivey is generally spineless when dealing with Nurse Ratched, because his job depends on the hospital's administrator, a woman who is an exArmy friend of Nurse Ratched's. Dr. Spivey finds McMurphy as amusing as the patients do, and discovers that he and McMurphy attended the same high school. He begins to assert his authority as a doctor, sticking up for the patients when they want to continue their basketball games and joining them on the hilarious fishing trip set up by McMurphy.

Candy Starr

McMurphy's prostitute friend who joins the patients and the doctor on the fishing trip and later at McMurphy's final jaunt, the party. She has sex with Billy Bibbit, which leads to tragedy. Her stereotypical portrayal as a "hooker with a heart of gold" has led some critics to call the book sexist.

Maxwell Wilson Taber

A patient who is forcibly given a shot of medicine after he questions what is in it. Chief Bromden pictures him as a success story—a "Dismissal" who returns to the community, readjusted from his stay at the hospital.

Mr. Turkle

An older black man who is an orderly on the night shift. He treats the patients kindly, even though he fears if he is discovered he might be fired. He cooperates with McMurphy's plans to have a party on the ward, but resigns the next day after things get out of hand.

Mr. Warren

See The Three Black Boys

Mr. Washington

See The Three Black Boys

Mr. Williams

See The Three Black Boys

Individual vs. Society

The main action of *One Flew Over the Cuckoo's Nest* consists of McMurphy's struggles against the strict rules of Big Nurse Ratched. Her ward at the hospital is a society in itself, for it has its own laws and punishments, both for the inmates and for the orderlies and nurses who watch over them. McMurphy challenges the rules from the time he arrives, from upsetting the supposedly "democratic" procedure of group therapy to brushing his teeth before the appointed time. By having McMurphy question and ridicule Nurse Ratched's ludicrous, controlling rules, Kesey portrays the individual's struggle against a conformist society as a noble, meaningful task. McMurphy's fight within the small world of the hospital can also be extended to the outside world. During the time Kesey was writing the novel, society emphasized conformity as a means of upholding law and order. Through the portrayal of one individual's meaningful fight against a small society, Kesey brought into question the standards of his own society at large.

Sanity and Insanity

One of society's standards provides the most pervasive theme in the book: What is sane—and what is insane? Is sanity conformance with society and its norms? Or is sanity a sense of self as separate from society? These are questions that psychiatrists have wrestled with for over a century. Is it their job to reprogram a person to fit better into what may be an unsatisfactory life or a flawed society? Or is it their responsibility to guide a person toward self-realization, no matter how that differs from the norm of the patient's environment?

In portraying McMurphy's struggles on the Acute/Chronic Ward, Kesey questions his society's definitions of sanity, which seem to ask all people to conform to the same standards of behavior. When McMurphy discovers that many of the Acutes are at the hospital voluntarily, he wants to know why: "You, you're not exactly the everyday man on the street, but you're not *nuts.*" Billy Bibbit replies that they don't have the "guts" to get along in outside society, but ironically, Nurse Ratched's methods are designed to undermine the men's confidence, not encourage it. In this way, Kesey portrays his society's definition of "madness" as something used by an authoritarian culture to dehumanize the individual and replace it with an automaton that dwells in a safe, blind conformity. His hero, McMurphy, is the person who sees through this sham. By showing his fellow patients how to create their own standards of sanity, McMurphy leads a bunch of institutionalized robots back towards their humanity. In the process, he suffers greatly and in fact lays down his life.

Sacrifice

McMurphy's struggle against Nurse Ratched, although eventually lost, is shown to be a sacrifice which liberates his fellow inmates. As Scanlon encourages Chief Bromden to escape at the end of the novel, he says that McMurphy "showed you how one time, if you think back." Reinforcing this theme of sacrifice are the recurring images of crucifixion that appear throughout the book. Consider the pathetic character of the mind-destroyed Chronic Ellis, "nailed" in Chief's eyes to the wall behind which sinister wires and machinery hum. Or the cross-shaped table on which the victims of electroshock therapy lie. The image of the cross is repeated in Chief's description of the position in which Sefelt lies after he suffers an epileptic episode: "His hands are nailed out to each side with the palms up and the fingers jerking open and shut, just the way I've watched men jerk at the Shock Shop strapped to the crossed table, smoke curling up out of the palms from the current."

Topics for Further Study

- Write a short essay or story on what would happen if McMurphy took a job in a large corporation with a formal culture and a hierarchical structure. Be imaginative. Create characters who represent a variety of corporate types (the boss, the flatterer, the slacker, the busybody). Do not change McMurphy's personality, character, or behavior.

- Research the definitions of various mental illnesses, such as schizophrenia. Was McMurphy mentally ill or just a maverick who didn't fit into structured society? Defend your point of view with facts and illustrations.

- If you consider McMurphy to be a

hero, how would you categorize Chief Bromden? Defend your points with facts and illustrations from the book, and compare him to other characters in the book.

- Research current laws concerning mental illness and criminal prosecution. Explain how a person might be classified as "mentally ill" and prosecuted under current law, and explain whether or not McMurphy would have received the same sentencing today.

Point of View

Kesey seems to follow a fairly straightforward course in unfolding the plot of *One Flew Over the Cuckoo's Nest*. Except for a few flashbacks and digressions, the story is essentially told from beginning to end. The first-person ("I") narrator Chief Bromden, however, is a schizophrenic—a person prone to hallucinations and delusions. As a result, the reader is sometimes unsure whether some of the events he describes really happened or not. After all, Chief believes he sees small mechanical items inside the capsules of medicine he receives and believes that a machine is responsible for creating the "fog" that enfolds his perceptions. Having Chief as a narrator also adds to the development of the story, however, for told through his eyes, the story unfolds in part through Chief's changing emotional and intellectual state. After McMurphy leads the revolt over the World Series, for example, Chief notes that "there's no more fog any place," implying that McMurphy is actually helping to bring sanity to the ward.

Setting

The setting plays a pivotal role in the novel, especially because it rarely changes. By keeping the action in one place—the Chronic/Acute Ward of a mental institution—Kesey is able to create a whole society in miniature. As the novel opens, this society is an ordered holding pen for men who have various degrees of mental illness. When the outsider McMurphy arrives, he brings the monotonous, repetitive qualities of this setting into focus. Only on one occasion does the action take place outside of the hospital, when the men go on the fishing party. With the vivid descriptions of this trip, the pace picks up as the men come alive. This provides further contrast to life on the ward, which is increasingly seen as cruel and dehumanizing. The author further enriches the setting with language that is strong, concrete, direct, and vivid. It brings the reader right into the midst of the action.

Characterization

The portrayal of the inmates of the institution, for the most part, are real and believable. Some are modeled on patients Kesey observed while doing night supervisory duty on a mental ward. For instance, the behavior of George Sorenson, known as "Rub-a-Dub," who is so concerned about cleanliness he won't touch anyone, is an example of obsessive-compulsive disorder. Especially moving is Chief's slow awakening to a validation of himself as a person, after experiencing years of racial slurs and physical degradation. The novel's portrayal of female and African American characters, however, is more problematic. Women are either control freaks who emasculate the men around them, such as Nurse Ratched, Vera Harding, and Billy Bibbit's mother, or objects for sexual gratification, such as the two hookers Candy and Sandy. The "black boys" Chief describes are alternately servile to their boss, Nurse Ratched, and cruel to the patients, showing no emotion but hatred. While Mr. Turkle's character is more sympathetic, he too is portrayed as fearful of authority and responsibility. While broad stereotypes such as these serve a purpose in creating a satire such as *Cuckoo's Nest*, they have still led to accusations of sexism and racism.

The 1950s: Conformity and Change

The late 1950s, the time period in which the book was written and set, saw the end of a decade in which people outside the mainstream were often viewed with suspicion. The United States was engaged in a "cold war" with the Soviet Union, in which relations were tense and hostile even though no open warfare was declared. Americans feared the possibility of a nuclear conflict, and people identified as communist sympathizers—"reds"—were frequently ostracized and even persecuted for their supposed beliefs by government committees such as that headed by Senator Joseph McCarthy. But toward the end of the decade, a national rebellion against civil injustice and cultural mediocrity was in the making. Young people in particular began questioning the values and beliefs of those in power. One such group of people were the Beat Generation, who expressed their dissatisfaction with society through art, dress, and nonviolent action. Poetry readings were a common forum beatniks used to communicate their ideas, and Allen Ginsberg's 1955 poem "Howl" articulated what many people saw as the moral and social problems of the time.

Groups such as the Beat generation became

part of a larger movement known as the counterculture. What began as a band of political protesters eventually gave rise in the 1960s to the hippies, a group dedicated to peace, love, and the quest to expand one's inner horizons through the use of mind-altering drugs such as LSD. Kesey's experiences bridged the two groups, for he was a subject in a scientific experiment on the effects of LSD— lysergic acid diethylamide-25, one of the most potent mind-altering chemicals known. The drug had been discovered in 1938 by the Swiss chemist Dr. Albert Hofmann, and scientists determined that when carefully regulated, LSD was nonfatal and could even be used in the treatment of such psychological disorders as schizophrenia. In treating these disorders, however, successful results were often marred by the sometimes dramatic and unpleasant reactions—usually manifested in visual and/or audible hallucinations—that would accompany them. To the rising counterculture of the 1960s, LSD served as a way to help explore their own minds and expand their horizons. However, the hallucinations could induce aggressive, even dangerous, behavior in users, who also were prone to uncontrollable "flashback" episodes. LSD has been a controlled substance—illegal to make, distribute, sell, or possess—since 1966, and Kesey himself has since disavowed the use of drugs, saying that the costs far exceed the benefits.

Mental Illness and Its Treatment

For many years in the United States, mental

illness was often ignored or misinterpreted; treatment often consisted of nothing more than chaining or caging the sufferer. During the mid-1800s, attitudes regarding the mentally ill slowly began to change. Thanks to the efforts of humanitarian reformers such as Dorothea Dix, millions of dollars were raised to establish state mental institutions capable of caring for large numbers of patients. After World War II, when more soldiers were medically discharged because of neuropsychiatric disorders than for any other reason, the medical community began to more closely evaluate the conditions that existed in the mental health care system.

Compare & Contrast

- **Early 1960s:** In 1962, the Cold War reaches its most fevered pitch during the Cuban Missile Crisis. U.S. President John F. Kennedy imposes a naval blockade on Cuba after discovering evidence of Soviet missile construction on the island, and the U.S.S.R. goes on special military alert.

  Today: The Soviet Union no longer exists, and Russia, the largest country left from the Soviet breakup, has a democratically elected president. The Russian government's biggest problems are paying their military, funding the government, and rising organized crime.

- **Early 1960s:** After the government shuts down official studies of LSD in the late 1950s, research into the effects of the hallucinogenic drug is carried on at a few universities. The drug, still legal, becomes popular with young people, particularly members of the "counterculture."
Today: A controlled substance since 1966, LSD is illegal throughout the United States. Although its popularity has largely been replaced by drugs like cocaine and heroin, its use has increased over the last decade.

- **Early 1960s:** New thinking on the nature of mental illness—that it might not be medically related to the brain—leads to a decrease in the number of institutionalized patients. Where in 1955 half of all hospital beds were occupied by the mentally ill, over the next two decades there is a 65% reduction in the number of mental patients, many of whom end up on the street.
Today: Many forms of mental illness, such as schizophrenia, have been traced to malfunctions in specific areas of the brain.

Researchers have even located the genes which, if defective, can lead to certain types of mental illness. In 1997, the National Coalition for the Homeless estimated that 20–25% of all homeless people have some form of mental illness.

In the 1950s, advances in pharmaceuticals led to more methods of treatment for mental patients; in 1956, more patients were being discharged from U.S. mental institutions than admitted for the first time in over a century, many aided by prescribed drugs to manage irrational behavior. In addition to medication, the use of electroshock therapy and psychosurgery were common treatments for psychiatric disorders. Electroshock therapy, or ECT, was discovered in 1937 by two Italian psychiatrists who thought to apply an electrical charge directly to the brain. Despite the harsh stigma that has been unfairly associated with this type of treatment—in Kesey's novel it is seen as a means of punishment rather than a cure—the use of electroshock therapy has proven immensely successful in cases involving moderate to severe bouts of depression. Others argue that its side effects make it one of the more barbaric forms of legal medical procedures in the modern age.

A third mode of treatment, and by far the most controversial, is the destruction of certain cells or fibers in the brain through surgical measures. At the onset, this technique was labeled a "lobotomy" because it required the removal of the frontal lobe of the brain. Later, with modern, more precise means of locating desired tissues, it is more commonly referred to as psychosurgery. The first lobotomy on record was performed in the United States in 1936 by Dr. Walter Freeman. Although original results proved successful in calming down patients with highly energetic or exceedingly violent personalities, soon physicians began noticing undesirable effects on the patient's mental and physical health. These effects are epitomized by Kesey's character McMurphy after his experience in undergoing such surgery.

Critical Overview

When *One Flew Over the Cuckoo's Nest* was published in 1962, it was well received by the critics and swiftly gained popularity among college-age readers. Critic Malcolm Cowley, one of Kesey's teachers at Standard, commented in a letter to Kesey that the book (which he read in rough draft) contained "some of the most brilliant scenes I have ever read" and "passion like I've not seen in young writers before." R. A. Jelliffe, writing in the *Chicago Sunday Tribune Magazine of Books*, praised the novel for its brilliant mixture of realism and myth, noting "this is an allegory with a difference." *Time* magazine praised Kesey for both his power and humor, describing the book as "a strong, warm story about the nature of human good and evil, despite the macabre setting." While some initial reviews faulted the novel as rambling, the majority agreed with *New York Times Book Review* contributor Martin Levin that *Cuckoo's Nest* was "a work of genuine literary merit."

It wasn't long after the novel appeared, however, that criticism arose over its negative portrayal of female characters. Julian Moynahan, for instance, argued in a 1964 *New York Review of Books* article that *Cuckoo's Nest* was "a very beautiful and inventive book violated by a fifth-rate idea which made Woman, in alliance with modern technology, the destroyer of masculinity and sensuous enjoyment." Similarly, Marcia L. Falk criticized the popular acceptance of the work and its Broadway adaptation in a 1971 letter to the *New York Times*. She noted that people "never even noticed, or cared to question, the psychic disease out of which the book's vision was born." Other critics have defended the work by noting, for instance, that the negative female stereotypes are there to support the novel's satire or that these negative characters are not truly representatives of women, but rather representatives of evil. Either way, the novel has inspired many articles analyzing how it portrays gender conflict and defines masculinity and humanity in general. As Richard D. Maxwell wrote in *Twenty-Seven to One:* "It is apparent that Kesey is not putting the entire blame [on women for men's loss of power].... It is the male who is allowing the female and the corporation to chip away at his masculinity."

Another debated aspect of the novel has been its portrayal of racial groups, specifically the black orderlies who work on the ward. Chief expresses hatred for these men, who are little more than stupid and cruel stereotypes, and he and McMurphy often express their anger with racial slurs. Several critics have pointed out, however, that these men are seen through the mind of the Chief, who himself has been the victim of prejudice as well as the "Combine" that dehumanizes people of all races. In this fashion Chief's racial observations create an ironic commentary on the nature of racism, as Janet R. Sutherland remarked in *English Journal:* "Just as the reader has to look beyond the typically racist language of the inmate to find in the book as a whole a document of witness against the dehumanizing, sick effects of racism in our society, so Bromden has to look beyond the perception of the world which limits his concept of self."

A large number of articles have examined how the novel defines the role of the hero in a society which stifles individuality, and who exactly is the hero of the novel. While some observers have argued that McMurphy, who through his example and sacrifice shows the men how to escape, is the hero, many others suggest that it is Chief Bromden who is ultimately the hero of the work. While McMurphy leads his "disciple" Bromden to a new understanding, Barry H. Leeds noted in *Connecticut Review*, "it is not until the very end of the novel … that it becomes clear that Bromden has surpassed his teacher in the capacity to survive in American society." Ronald Wallace likewise argued in his *The Last Laugh* that Bromden rejects the "extreme" of total freedom and chaos that McMurphy represents and "has recreated himself in his own best image: strong, independent, sensitive, sympathetic, and loving, with a comic perspective on his human limitations." In the *Rocky Mountain Review of Language and Literature*, Thomas H. Fick placed Bromden's triumph as the hero in the tradition of the mythology of the American West, where a Native American guides a white man to greater understanding. Kesey has turned this myth on its side, noted Fick, creating "the first [instance], surely, that the Indian partner in such a pair has outlived his White brother." The result, concluded the critic, is "a powerful novel which effectively translates into contemporary terms the enduring American concern with a freedom found only in— or in between—irreconcilable oppositions."

Sources

Marcia L. Falk, in a letter to the New York Times, December 5, 1971, reprinted in One Flew Over the Cuckoo's Nest: Text and Criticism by Ken Kesey, edited by John Clark Pratt, Viking, 1973, pp. 450–53.

Thomas H. Fick, "The Hipster, the Hero, and the Psychic Frontier in 'One Flew Over the Cuckoo's Nest," in Rocky Mountain Review ofLanguage and Literature, Vol. 43, Nos. 1–2, 1989, pp. 19–32.

R. A. Jelliffe, review of One Flew over the Cuckoo's Nest, in Chicago Sunday Tribune, February 4, 1962, p. 3.

Barry H. Leeds, 'Theme and Technique in One Flew Over the Cuckoo's Nest," in Connecticut ReviewVol. 7, No. 2, April, 1974, pp. 35–50.

Martin Levin, review of One Flew over the Cuckoo's Nest, in New York Times Book Review, February 4, 1962, p. 32.

Richard D. Maxwell, "The Abdication of Masculinity in One Flew Over the Cuckoo's Nest," in Twenty-Seven to One, edited by Bradford C. Broughton, Ryan Press, 1970, pp. 203–11.

Julian Moynahan, "Only in America," in New York Review of Books, Vol. III, No. 2, September 10, 1964, pp. 14–15.

A review of One Flew over the Cuckoo's Nest, in

Time, Vol. 79, February 16, 1962, p. 90.

Janet Sutherland, "A Defense of Ken Kesey's 'One Flew Over the Cuckoo's Nest,'" in English Joumal, Vol. 61, No. 1, January, 1972, pp. 28–31.

Ronald Wallace, "What Laughter Can Do: Ken Kesey's 'One Flew Over the Cuckoo's Nest,'" in his The Last Laugh: Form andAffirrmation in the Contemporary American Comic Novel, University of Missouri Press, 1979, pp. 90–114.

For Further Study

John A. Barsness, "Ken Kesey: The Hero in Modern Dress," in *Bulletin of the Rocky Mountain Modern Language Association*, Vol. 23, No. 1, March, pp. 27–33.

> Argues that the novel is an updated version of the Westem and its cowboy hero.

Annette Benert, "The Forces of Fear: Kesey's Anatomy of Insanity," in *Lex et Scientia* Vol. 13, Nos. 1–2, January-June, 1977, pp. 22–26.

> Analyzes the novel's connections to fear of woman, fear of the machine, and glorification of the hero.

Robert Boyers, "Pomo-Politics," in *The Annals of the American Academy of Political and Social Sciences*, No. 376, March, 1968, pp. 36–52.

> Examines the novel's attitudes towards sex and the linkages between sexuality and laughter.

Leslie A. Fiedler, in his *The Retum of the Vanishing American*, Stein & Day, 1968.

> Fiedler's views on the mythic relationships in *Cuckoo's Nest* are almost as well-known as the novel itself.

Benjamin Goluboff, "The Carnival Artist in The

Cuckoo's Nest," in *Northwest Review*, Vol. 29, No. 3, 1991, pp. 109–122.

A contemporary reading of the novel employing the Russian critic Mikhail Bakhtin's ideas of the carnivalesque.

Leslie Horst, "Bitches, Twitches, and Eunuchs: Sex-Role Failure and Caricature," in *Lex et Scientia* Vol. 13, Nos. 1–2, January-June, 1977, pp. 14–17.

This essay frankly confronts the novel's narrow portrayals of sex roles, both masculine and feminine.

Ken Kesey, *Kesey's Garage Sale*, Viking, 1973.

Contains stories and interviews, as well as a screenplay.

Ken Kesey, *One Flew Over the Cuckoo's Nest: Text and Criticism by Ken Kesey*, edited by John Clark Pratt, Viking, 1973, pp. 450–53.

An edition of the novel that includes reprints of important early critical essays on the novel.

Irving Malin, "Ken Kesey: 'One Flew Over The Cuckoo's Nest,'" in *Critique*, Vol. 5, No. 2, 1962, pp. 81–84.

Irving's essay situates the novel in the mode of the New American Gothic, which "gives us violent juxtapositions, distorted vision, even prophecy."

Carol Pearson, "The Cowboy Saint and the Indian

Poet: The Comic Hero in Ken Kesey's 'One Flew Over the Cuckoo's Nest,'" in *Studies in American Humor*, Vol. 1, No. 2, October, 1974, pp. 91–98.

> Employs the myth of the king, the hero, and fool to an understanding of the novel.

M. Gilbert Porter, *One Flew Over the Cuckoo's Nest: Rising to Heroism*, Twayne Masterwork Studies No. 22, Twayne, 1989.

> A book-length study of Kesey's novel which explores the concept of heroism in the novel.

Terry G. Sherwood, "'One Flew Over the Cuckoo's Nest' and the Comic Strip," in *Critique*, Vol. 13, No. 1, 1971, pp. 96–109.

> A clever analysis of the role of comic books and comic book figures in the novel.

Joseph J. Waldmeir, "Two Novels of the Absurd: Heller and Kesey," in *Wisconsin Studies in Contemporary Literature*, Vol. 5, No. 3, 1964, pp. 192–204.

> This essay argues that Kesey's novel is in fact a better example of the absurd than Heller's *Catch-22*.

Tom Wolfe, *The Electric Kool-Aid Acid Test*, Farrar, Strauss, 1968.

> Wolfe's "New Joumalism" novel about Kesey and the Merry

Pranksters.

CPSIA information can be obtained
at www.ICGtesting.com
Printed in the USA
LVOW13s1746311017
554455LV00010B/604/P